Reginald Dixon was born in 1910 in Staffc
Gloucester since 1950. He served in the R
World War, and retired from a career on the staff of the National
Bank in 1970. He first started seeking out and photographing 'curiosities'
more than fifty years ago, and has contributed his findings to nearly 200
different periodicals over the years.

Frontispiece: The round house at Chalford built in 1790 as a
watchtower for the Thames and Severn Canal (see No. 56).

Cotswold Curiosities

Reginald Dixon

THE DOVECOTE PRESS

First published in 1988 by The Dovecote Press Ltd
Stanbridge, Wimborne, Dorset BH21 4JD
ISBN 0 946159 51 1

© Reginald Dixon 1988

Photoset in Palatino by Character Graphics, Taunton, Somerset
Printed and bound by Biddles Ltd, Guildford and King's Lynn

Contents

Cotswold Curiosities

PERSHORE EVESHAM

BROADWAY MORETON-IN-MARSH

CHIPPING NORTON

STOW-ON-THE-WOLD

TEWKESBURY

CHELTENHAM BURFORD

GLOUCESTER

PAINSWICK CIRENCESTER LECHLADE

STROUD

DURSLEY TETBURY

MALMESBURY

YATE

CHIPPENHAM

MILES

0   10

BRISTOL BATH

Introduction

Ever since I can remember I have been attracted by the odd and peculiar; and when I see an unsual building or object I immediately start wondering who built it, when and why. I hope that sense of inquisitiveness will never leave me. It is said that 'curiosity killed the cat', but I am no cat, and although nearly eighty years old remain as curious as ever.

When I took up photography in 1934 it was only natural that I should photograph the curiosities I came across, and over the years I have amassed a large collection. Sadly, many of those items I first photographed have since vanished, but those that survive remain a delightful testament to the enduring streak of eccentricity in the British character.

What constitutes a curiosity? For me, it is anything out of the ordinary, from an unusal building to a peculiarly shaped tree. Objects not particularly unsual in appearance may qualify as curiosities because they are the biggest, smallest, or oldest of their kind; or have some unique feature. Again, an object may have an interesting story connected with it.

During the years I have lived in Gloucester I have found the Cotswolds a veritable treasure house of curiosities, and in this book I have assembled a collection that sums up their diversity. They are presented in a manner which allows the curiosity seeker to find them easily, and I have added notes on the chief points of interest.

The 'Cotswolds' is a rather loosely defined area, but for my own purposes I have included the countryside stretching from Bristol and Bath in the south to Chipping Campden in the north east and nearly as far north as Evesham. It is a glorious landscape, as residents know, but visitors will not be disappointed by the villages and countryside through which they pass in search of the curiosities I have chosen.

I would finally like to record my thanks to my friend Bob George for suggesting that I record my findings in a book, and putting me in touch with David Burnett of the Dovecote Press.

1 Oddities at Cleeve Prior

Position: 2 miles S.W. of Bidford-on-Avon
Ordnance Map: Worcester and The Malverns; Sheet 150 1:50 000
Map Ref: 0870/4930
Access: From Bidford-on-Avon take the B4085 going southwards.
After ½ mile turn left for Marlcliff and Cleeve Prior.

Note: In the Middle Ages churchyards were the venue for all sorts
of village activities, including archery practice. At Cleeve Prior, on
the south west butress of the tower can be seen the grooves in the
stonework where they sharpened their arrows. South of the tower
is a tombstone in memory of Sara Charlett who, according to the
inscription, died in 1693 at the age of 309. A yew tree near the
south door is said to be over 600 years old.

Inside the church, when I called, there was an ancient wooden
cradle beside the 14th century font. The elm chest, over 8 ft. long
and hewn from a solid tree trunk, is probably 14th century.

Places of interest in the Neighbourhood
At Rous Lench there are two letter boxes housed in special
timbered shelters. They were erected by Dr. Chaffy, a 19th century
parson-squire anxious to preserve the rural appearance of the
village. They are both still in use.
4. The Missing Castle (Elmley Castle)

Food and Accommodation
Available at Bidford-on-Avon.

2 "Wee-Wee Cottage"

Position: In the village of Wyre Piddle, two miles N. East of Pershore
Ordnance Map: Worcester and The Malverns; Sheet 150 1:50 000
Map Ref: 9620/4760
Access: Enter Wyre Piddle by the B4083 from Pershore. Wee Wee cottage is opposite the rear of the Post office, in Worcester Road close to where the B4083 joins the B4084.

Note: If you are looking for a public convenience do not be misled by the sign on this door. It is just an ordinary private dwelling.

Places of interest in the Neighbourhood
1. Oddities at Cleeve Prior (Cleeve Prior)
3. A Remarkable Church Gateway (Birlingham)
4. The Missing Castle (Elmley Castle)

Food and Accommodation
Available at the Avonside Hotel nearby and some houses display B & B signs. Food is also available at The Anchor Inn.

3 A Remarkable Church Gateway

Position: At Birlingham, 2 miles south of Pershore
Ordnance Map: Worcester and The Malverns; Sheet 150 1.50 000
Map Ref: 9320/4310
Access: Take the A4104 leading southwards from Pershore. After
1¼ miles take the minor road on your left for Birlingham.

Note: When Birlingham church was rebuilt in the Victorian era the
12th century chancel archway was re-erected over the churchyard
gate. Recently the church has been bothered by the invasion of
bats whose droppings foul the pews. In an effort to scare them off a
stuffed owl has been placed on a windowledge. Whether or not this
proves effective remains to be seen.

Places of interest in the Neighbourhood
  2. "Wee Wee Cottage" (Wyre Piddle)
  4. The Missing Castle (Elmley Castle)
 11. Helping Hands at the Crossroads (Teddington Hands)

Food and Accommodation
Plenty in Pershore.

The model of Elmley Castle.

4 The Missing Castle

Position: At the southern end of Elmley Castle village, 3 miles
S.W. of Evesham
Ordnance Map: Worcester and The Malverns; Sheet 150 1:50 000
Map Ref: 9820/4100
Access: From Evesham take the A435 running southwards. After
1¾ miles (at Hinton Cross) turn right for Elmley Castle.

Note: Visitors to the village of Elmley Castle often wonder why
they cannot see any sign of a castle. The answer is that the castle,
built about 1086 by Robert D'Abitot, no longer exists. It fell into
bad need of repair from the time of Henry VII onwards and was
used as a quarry by local builders. All that now remains are the
earthern ramparts and ditches.

However, if you enter the church you can see a model of the
castle as it used to be. This was made many years ago by Percy
Gibson, a local man, from faded drawing and plans found in the
church deed box. The model used to be in the nave but has now
been moved to the tower.

In the church porch is a quaint medieval carving of a rabbit, and
in the churchyard are two multi faced sundials dating from about

1550. The Queen Elizabeth Inn, close to the church, has a sign depicting the arrival of Queen Elizabeth I arriving at the village in 1575.

Places of interest in the Neighbourhood
3. A Remarkable Church Gateway (Birlingham)
6. A Pair of Stones (Beckford)
11. Helping Hands at the Crossroads (Teddington Hands)

Food: Available at The Old Mill Inn in Elmley Castle.
Accommodation: Plenty at Evesham or Pershore.

Elizabethan sundial in Elmley Castle churchyard.

5 A Tithe Barn and a Tomb

Position: At Bredon on the B4080, North East of Tewkesbury
Ordnance Map: Worcester and The Malverns; Sheet 150 1.50 000
Map Ref: 9200/3690
Access: From the main road at Tewkesbury end of the village.

Note: The Tithe Barn, dating from 1350, is one of the best
preserved in the country and is in the care of The National Trust.
The outside can be inspected at any time, and entrance to the
inside can be obtained between March and September. The barn is
about 50 yards long and massive wooden pillars inside support the
roof. External stone steps lead to the bailiff's office which is
equipped with a fireplace, and a hole leading to a cesspit for use as
a lavatory.

The nearby church is worth a visit for the Crusader's Tomb
containing the heart of Sir Nicholas de Mitton, killed on a Crusade
in the Holy Land.

In the Middle Ages when important people died a long way from
home they were often buried locally but their hearts removed and
taken to their home church for interment. Sometimes the body was
boiled in wine so that the bones could be separated from the flesh
for separate burial.

There is a magnificent tomb of Sir Giles Reed, and his helmet
hangs on the wall near by.

Places of interest in the Neighbourhood
  6. A Pair of Stones (Beckford)
 10. Tewkesbury's Historic Inns
 16. Saxon Relics at Deerhurst

Food and Accommodation
Available at The Fox & Hounds near to the Northern entrance of
the church.

6 A Pair of Stones

Position: Beckford, 5½ miles north east of Tewkesbury
Ordnance Map: Worcester and The Malverns; Sheet 150 1.50 000
Map Ref: 9750/3560
Access: There is a pleasant rural route between Bredon and Elmley
Castle via Kemerton, Overbury, Beckford and Aston-under-Hill.
Most of the churches passed provide some items of interest.

Note: At Overbury, for example, in the churchyard is an epitaph to
Elizabeth Smith who died in 1821.

> "Adieu dear husband, I am past.
> I loved you while my life did last.
> Now for me do not sorrow take,
> But love my children for my sake".

Arriving at Beckford from Overbury the first thing to catch one's
eye is a remarkable pillar mile stone, about 15 feet tall. One face is
inscribed "ELIZABETH II CORONATION" but this was added
at the time of the coronation and the stone itself is much older. It
was erected in 1887 to commemorate Queen Victoria's Jubilee.
Originally it was surrounded by iron railings, but these were
removed during the drive for scrap metal during the 2nd World
War. When Elizabeth II was crowned the original inscription on
the base was cement rendered over and the new inscription added.

In Beckford churchyard, just to the right of the church porch as
you enter, is a headstone in memory of Sarah Dyer who died in
1838. The inscription reads:

> "She was daily letter carrier from
> Beckford to Tewkesbury for 19 years
> and having walked about 16 miles a
> day during that period is supposed
> to have walked about 90,000 miles".

Places of interest in the Neighbourhood
   4. The Missing Castle (Elmley Castle)
   5. A Tithe Barn and a Tomb (Bredon)
  11. Helping Hands at the Crossroads (Teddington Hands)

Food and Accommodation
Available in most of the villages.

7 Bier at Broadway Old Church

Position: South of Broadway village
Ordnance Map: Worcester and The Malverns; Sheet 150 1.50 000
Map Ref: 0970/3620
Access: From Broadway take the road to Snowshill. After ¾ mile you will come to the ancient church of St. Eadburgha.

Note: The church contains a most unusual bier with solid wooden wheels. It was presented to the church in 1888 in memory of Charles Smart (vicar for 25 years). There is also an interesting pillar Alms Box with 3 locks, one for the vicar and each church warden. It is believed to date from about the year 1200.

Places of interest in the Neighbourhood
Snowshill Manor (A National Trust Property containing a fascinating collection of ancient clocks mechanical toys, agricultural implements etc.)
  8. Broadway Tower
13. Memories of J. N. Barrie (Stanway)
79. The Man who Rescued Robinson Crusoe (Stanway)

Food and Accommodation
Plenty in Broadway

8 Broadway Tower

Position: ¾ mile south of Broadway
Ordnance Map: Worcester and The Malverns; Sheet 150 1.50 000
Map Ref: 1130/3620
Access: From the A44, 1½ miles east of Broadway, take the minor road leading south west up Broadway Hill. After ½ mile you will see the 65 ft. tall tower on your right.

Note: This imposing folly was built in the 18th century by the 6th Earl of Coventry, and it is claimed that on a clear day it is possible

to see 13 counties from the top. When the Earl married, his bride saw the hill and thought it might be visible from her family home at Croom Court, near Worcester. A beacon was lit to prove her right, and Lord Coventry had the tower built to please her.

After renovation work was carried out in 1827 it was used as a dwelling house by various people. William Morris, the Pre-Raphaelite designer, poet, painter and social reformer used the tower for extended holidays. Other famous people who stayed there include the artist Edward Burne-Jones, and Dante Gabriel Rossetti the poet.

The tower is now the centre of a country park open to the public daily from April to early October, 10.00 to 18.00. In addition to the magnificent views there are exhibitions in the tower, a nature trail, and an adventure playground.

Places of interest in the Neighbourhood
7. Bier at Broadway Old Church.
9. An Impatient Virgin and an Honest Man (Chipping Campden)
12. A Fishy Story (Blockley)

Food and Accommodation
Available near the tower during the summer, in Broadway at all times.

The Kiftsgate Stone.

9 An Impatient Virgin and an Honest Man

Position: Chipping Campden churchyard
Ordnance Map: Stratford-upon-Avon; Sheet 151 1.50 000
Map Ref: 1550/3960

Note: In Chipping Campden churchyard are two interesting head
stones close to the table tomb near the church door. In memory of
Marther Hiron ? (name indistinct), who died in 1708, aged 41. –

> "Here lieth a virgin pure and chaste
> Who did not want her time to waste
> She dearly longed to married be
> To Christ her Lord and none but he
> And now she has her soul at rest
> With glorious sounds for ever blest."

In memory of Richard Tinley who died in January 1860.

> "Here a man who kept his word
> As far as mortals could
> To grieve for him would be absurd
> Because his life was good.
> He lived and died an honest man
> Go then and do the same
> Twill recommend the Gospel plan
> And yield thee endless fame."

Another curiosity in the neighbourhood is the Kiftsgate Stone with
a hole in it where the chief of the Saxon Hundred stuck his sword
when collecting dues from serfs. It was here that they came to pay
homage and get counsel from the Saxon "Witan", the forerunner
of our parliament. The stone is situated ¾ mile west of Chipping
Campden on the road leading to Willersley. It is amongst some
trees, just inside a gap in the hedge on the right hand side of the
road.

Food and Accommodation
Plenty in Chipping Campden.

10 Tewkesbury's Historic Inns

Ordnance Map: Worcester and The Malverns; Sheet 150 1.50 000
Map Ref: 8950/3250

Note: In addition to its famous Abbey Tewkesbury has many
interesting old buildings, including some historic Inns. These
include the following in the main Street. "The Black Bear", which
dates from 1308 and is the oldest Inn in Gloucestershire: "The
Royal Hop Pole Inn", where Dicken's Mr. Pickwick stopped to
dine: "The Tudor House", part of which dates from 1540, and has
a staircase leading to an attic where Charles II is said to have
hidden after the Battle of Worcester. Leading to the garden is a
large oak gate of unusual design bearing the strange inscription
"Antiquity Walks Hand in Hand with Time and still retains its
dignity – There is Peace. – 1540 – 1932". On the outskirts of the
town (A38 towards Gloucester) is "Gupshill Manor Hotel" from
which Queen Margaret watched the Battle of Tewkesbury in 1471.

Other interesting buildings in the town include two which are
often missed because of their obscure position. One is the 19th
century mill which featured in the famous novel *John Halifax
Gentleman* at the end of Mill Street, opposite the Abbey. Nearby,
in Old Baptist Chapel Court, is a very old chapel. Originally a 15th
century house it was converted to a chaple in 1623 and is open to
the public. In Barton Street is a small but very interesting Folk
Museum.

Places of interest in the Neighbourhood
  5. A Tithe Barn and Tomb (Bredon)
 16. Saxon Relics at Deerhurst

Food and Accommodation
Plenty in Tewkesbury.

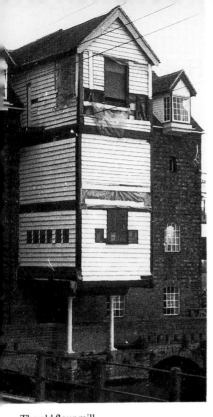

The old flour mill.

'Ye Olde Black Bear'.

Guphill Manor Hotel.

11 Helping Hands at the Crossroads

Position: At Teddington Hands, between Evesham and
Cheltenham, where the A438 and A435 cross
Ordnance Map: Worcester and The Malverns; Sheet 150 1.50 000
Map Ref: 9640/3380
Access: The post is close to the A435 about 100 yards west of the
roundabout.

Note: In olden days sign posts often had arms ending in a hand with
a finger pointing the direction. They were usually referred to as
"Finger Posts". Few now remain. This example marked the spot
where five roads met. It still retains its original form but a few years
ago it had to be moved 25 yards to make room for road
improvements. The post bears a small metal plaque inscribed as
follows.

> "Edmund Attwood of the Vine Tree
> At the first time erected me
> And freely he did this bestow
> Strange travellers the way to show
> Since generations past and gone
> Repaired by Charles Attwood of Teddington".

An old deed dated 1606 refers to Edmund Attwood,
husbandman of Teddington.

Places of interest in the Neighbourhood
  5. A Tithe Barn and a Tomb (Bredon)
  6. A Pair of Stones (Beckford)
 10. Tewkesbury's Historic Inns

Food: Available at Teddington Hands Inn close to the post.
Accommodation: Plenty in Tewkesbury

12 A Fishy Story

Position: At Blockley, 2½ miles south of Chipping Campden
Ordnance Map: Stratford-upon-Avon; Sheet 151 1.50 000
Map Ref: 1620/3450
Access: From the Dovedale end of the High Street.

Note: In the garden of Fish Cottage there is a memorial tablet in memory of a trout which lived over 100 years ago. It was kept by William Keyte who trained it to come to the surface to be fed. When the fish died in 1865 Keyte's son Charles inscribed an oak tablet which is sited close to the pond where the fish used to live. It reads:

> "Under the soil
> The old fish do lie.
> 20 years he lived
> And then did die.
> He was so tame
> You understand
> He would come and
> eat out of our hand.
>
> Died April 20th 1865
> Aged 20 Years.

It is also interesting to note that in the 19th century Joanna Southcott, the prophetess, lived at Rock Cottage in Blockley where she is said to have been consulted by no less a person than George IV. Unfortunately Rock Cottage was destroyed by fire in 1971.

Places of interest in the Neighbourhood
  9. An Impatient Virgin and an Honest Man (Chipping Campden)
 14. The Curfew Tower (Moreton-in-Marsh)
 15. The Four Shires Stone (Moreton-in-Marsh)

Food and Accommodation
Available in the village

13 Memories of J. M. Barrie

Position: At Stanway, 3 miles north west of Winchcombe
Ordnance Map: Worcester and The Malverns; Sheet 150 1.50 000
Map Ref: 0610/3230
Access: From the A438, where it meets the A46, take the B4077
towards Stow-on-the-Wold. After ¾ mile turn left to Stanway
village.

Note: J. M. Barrie, the celebrated author of *Peter Pan* visited
Stanway in 1921 when he was taken there by his secretary Cynthia
Asquith. She was the daughter of Lord and Lady Wemyss, owners
of Stanway House. Later he visited it on many occasions and came
to regard Stanway House as his second home.

  J. M. Barrie was a keen cricket enthusiast who once said he
thought its inventor a greater man than the author of *Hamlet*. He
formed his own cricket club in 1890. He called it "Allahakbars"
(Arabic for "Heaven Help us"). Its members included many many
well known authors such as Conan Doyle, Will Meredith, A. E. W.
Mason and P. G. Wodehouse.

The ground at Stanway is delightfully situated in a ridge and furrow field, and must be unique. The undulations extend into the outfield, but the pitch is level and maintained in excellent condition for village cricket. At one time an old railway carriage was used as a pavilion but J. M. Barrie paid for it to be replaced by an attractive rural construction raised on staddle stones. It remains to this day and was recently rethatched.

Anyone visiting Stanway cannot help being impressed by the magnificent Gate House at Stanway House. This is sometimes attributed wrongly to Inigo Jones. The house is open to the public on two afternoons a week during the months of June, July and August. It contains many interesting things but perhaps the most curious is an old wooden mouse trap in which the mouse is killed by a lead weight dropping on its head.

Places of interest in the Neighbourhood
7. Bier at Broadway Old Church (Broadway)
8. Broadway Tower
79. The Man who Rescued Robinson Crusoe (Stanway)

Food and Accommodation
Some available at near-by Stanton. Plenty at Winchcombe and Broadway.

The Curfew Tower and list of market tolls, **Moreton-in-Marsh.**

THE UNDERMENTION
TOLLS.
Will be charged in the Market Town of Moreton in on all market, fair and other days on and after this
Roundabouts driven by steam prohibite
For every Roundabout driven by pony   5s.to 6s.
"   Shooting Gallery.   . . .   5s.to 7s
"   Cocoanut Shoot. 2s
"   Cheap John Cart. 2s
"   Swing.   . . .   2s. 6d. to 5s
"   Waggon. . . .   . . .   1's.
"   Cart. . . .
"   Hand Cart. . . .
"   Stall of whatever length. . .
Id. per foot minimum.
For Earthenware Dealers 1s.for the use of 12
yards or less and for every additional yar
For every Show, Menagerie, Bazzar, &c.
hereinbefore mentioned Id. per square
For every Caravan accompanying any of the
Shows, Stalls, &c.and standing in the st
1's.per day, nothing to be allowed to st
within 18 feet of the Brick Pavemen
Residents having a stall in front of th
Houses 5s. per year.
BY ORDE
JOHN KENNEDY. Agent for,
THE RIGHT HON. LORD REDESDALE. K.C.V.O.
Lord of the Ma
F. PAGE
Collector

14 The Curfew Tower

Position: At Moreton-in-Marsh
Ordnance Map: Stratford-upon-Avon; Sheet 151 1.50 000
Map Ref: 2050/3240
Access: The Curfew Tower is in the main street on the corner of Oxford Street. There is a free car park by the railway station.

Note: This is one of the oldest buildings in the town and was erected in the 16th century. The bell, dated 1633, continued to be rung daily until 1860, probably as a result of a strange bequest. When Sir Robert Fry returned to Moreton-in-Marsh from London one foggy evening he got lost on the common. He eventually found his bearing upon hearing the sound of the curfew bell. In gratitude he left an endowment of £1 for winding the clock, which is dated 1648, and 10/- for ringing the bell. The bell was rung at 5 a.m. and 8 p.m. in summer, and at 6 a.m. and 8 p.m. in winter.

   On the wall is an interesting list of market tolls dated 5th August 1905, including such items as –

> Roundabouts driven by steam prohibited.
> Roundabouts drawn by pony 5/- to 6/- per day.
> Cheap John Cart 2/6 per day.
> Coconut shoot 2/6 per day.
> Stalls 1d per foot, minimum 6d per day.
> Earthenware Dealers for the use of 12
> square yards or less 1d per square yard.

Places of interest in the Neighbourhood
12. A Fishy Story (Blockley)
15. The Four Shires Stone (near Moreton-in-Marsh)
17. Succour for the Weary (Ford)

Food and Accommodation
Plenty in the town

15 The Four Shires Stone

Position: Beside the A44 where it is joined by the road from Great Wolford
Ordnance Map: Stratford-upon-Avon; Sheet 151 1.50 000
Map Ref: 2310/3210
Access: Take the A44 running eastwards from Moreton-in-Marsh. After 1¾ miles you will find the stone on your left.

Note: This stone pillar surmounted by a sundial and ball finial marks the spot where Gloucestershire, Oxfordshire and Warwickshire now meet. The names of these counties is inscribed on three faces of the pillar. The fourth is labelled Worcestershire, a reminder of the fact that before 20th century local government reform outlying parts of Worcestershire lay far south of the present county boundaries. In the 10th century Edward the Elder decided to carve up the western Midlands into administrative divisions called shires, each forming an easily defended block. They were based on the military centres of Warwick, Oxford, Gloucester and Worcester. He disregarded the boundaries of ancient kingdoms but took note of existing estate boundaries.

Places of interest in the Neighbourhood
12. A Fishy Story (Blockley)
14. The Curfew Tower (Moreton-in-Marsh)
18. The Rollright Stones (Long Compton)

Food and Accommodation
Plenty at Moreton-in-Marsh

16 Saxon Relics at Deerhurst

Position: 2 miles S.W. of Tewkesbury
Ordnance Map: Worcester and The Malverns; Sheet 150 1.50 000
Map Ref: 8700/2990
Access: From the A38 take the B4213 running westwards. After ½ mile take the right fork to Deerhurst.

Note: The Priory Church at Deerhurst is one of the most complete Saxon Buildings in England, and the font is described as the finest Saxon font in existance. Just across the road from the church is a Saxon Chapel dating from 1056 when it was erected by Earl Odda. The Priory Church is also well known for its fine brasses. Of particular interest is that showing Sir John Cassy and his wife. It measures 7ft. 5ins. by 3ft. and is located on the floor of the north aisle. At the feet of Lady Cassy it depicts a dog labled "Terri" and this is the only example in England of a brass showing a named pet.

Places of interest in the Neighbourhood
10. Tewkesbury's Historic Inns

Food: Available at Haw Bridge
Accommodation: Plenty at Tewkesbury

17 Succour for the Weary

Position: The village of Ford 4 miles N. East of Winchcombe
Ordnance Map: Worcester and The Malverns; Sheet 150 1.50 000
Map Ref: 0880/2940
Access: This tiny village is on the B4077 road from Broadway to
Stow-on-the Wold, and the inn is on the right hand side.

Note: On the outside wall of the Plough Inn at Ford you will find an
ancient sign reading as follows:

> "Ye weary travelers that pass by,
> With dust and scorching sunbeams dry
> Or be benumb'd with snow & frost,
> With having these bleak cotswolds crosst
> Step in and quaff my nut brown ale
> Bright as rubys mild and stale
> Twill make your laging trotters dance
> As nimble as the suns of france.
> Then ye will own ye men of sense
> That neare was better spent six pence."

You will still get a welcome at this inn, and they will provide you
with food and/or accommodation; but you are not likely to get a
pint of ale for six pence. The words "mild and stale" here have
their ancient meaning of "newly brewed, clear and strong".

Places of interest in the Neighbourhood
13. Memories of G. M. Barrie (Stanway)
19. Getting their own Back (Winchcombe)
79. The Man who Rescued Robinson Crusoe (Stanway)

Food and Accommodation
In addition to The Pough Inn there is plenty available in
Winchcombe.

18 The Rollright Stones

Position: About one mile south of Long Compton
Ordnance Map: Stratford-upon-Avon; Sheet 151 1.50 000
Map Ref: 2960/3090
Access: From Long Compton take the A34 towards Oxford. On the outskirts of the village fork right. After ¾ mile turn left and shortly left again. A few hundred yards further on you will see the King Stone close to the road on your left. The King's Men are almost opposite, on the other side of the road.

Note: The complex comprises three items.

(1) The King Stone. A single isolated stone 8ft tall. Bronze Age.
(2) The King's Men. A Bronze Age circle of 77 stones about 100 feet in diameter. These pitted and weathered stones vary in height from a few inches up to 7 feet.
(3) The Whispering Knights. Situated ¼ miles to the west, these include 4 Neolithic upright stones and a fallen capstone, once part of a burial chamber.

The King Stone.

The presence of these stones is accounted for by the following unlikely legend. An unnamed certain king set out to conquer England. At this spot he was met by a witch. When he consulted her about his prospects she answered , "Seven long strides shalt thou take, if Long Compton thou canst see then king of England though shalt be. If Long Compton thou cannot see then king of England thou shalt not be". Being close to the crest of the hill the king strode confidently forward, but reaching the top he found his view of Long Compton obscured by a large mound. The witch then turnéd the king and his men into stones, also a small group of knights who had separated from the main party and were whispering together plotting treason.

Places of interest in the Neighbourhood
22. The Itinerant Lady Rat Catcher (Chipping Norton)
23. The Remarkable Woollen Mill (Chipping Norton)

Food: At the Unicorn Inn, Great Rollright
Accommodation: Plenty at Chipping Norton

19 Getting their Own Back

Position: Winchcombe Church
Ordnance Map: Cheltenham & Cirencester; Sheet 163 1.50 000
Map Ref: 0240/2820
Access: From the main street.

Note: It is said that when the medieval masons were working on Winchcombe church they were annoyed by a monk from the nearby Abbey who criticised their work. In return they caricatured him in this grotesque gargoyle.

There are many interesting items inside the church. One of the most unusual is an ancient 'cello, which prior to 1868 was played regularly in the church at Gretton. There is also an altar cloth which includes embroidery done by Catherine of Aragon whilst she was staying at Sudeley Castle. The cloth was made from a 14th century priest's cope. Catherine added the surrounding border which is embroidered with her own pomegranate badge. The church has an usually fine weather cock measuring nearly 6 feet from beak to tail. It is made of wood and gilded. Originally at the

36

The seven leg stocks.

church of St Mary, Radcliffe, Bristol, it came to Winchcombe in 1872.

The old stocks, last used in 1860, can be seen at the corner of the High Street and North Street. It is interesting to see that it has an odd number of leg holes. Perhaps one of their regulars was a one legged man.

In 1932 Henry Ford tried to buy the church, planning to take it down, stone by stone, and rebuild it in America. He failed in this, but did succeed in getting the blacksmith's forge and a 17th century cottage from Chedworth. The operation was carried out with maticulous care, and involved the shipping of a flock of Cotswold sheep and a dovecote complete with the birds.

Places of interest in the Neighbourhood
Sudeley Castle
20. Belas Knap Long Barrow (Winchcombe)

Food and Accommodation
If you would like to take a meal at a fine timbered building where John Wesley accasionally stayed try the John Wesley Restaurant in the High Street. There are also many other restaurants and hotels in the town.

20 Belas Knap Long Barrow

Position: Two miles south of Winchcombe
Ordnance Map: Cheltenham & Cirencester; Sheet 163 1.50 000
Map Ref: 0180/2540
Access: From Winchcombe take the A46 towards Cheltenham but on the outskirts of Winchcombe turn left into Corndean Lane (signposted for Brockhampton and Andoversford). After about 1¼ miles leave car in lay-by on your left. Then follow the footpath opposite. This is well signposted and after about ¾ mile will bring you to the Long Barrow. Elderly people will find it a stiff climb.

Note: Belas Knap is a late Neolithic long barrow 170 feet long constructed about 1500 B.C. It has a false entrance at the end, to mislead would be robbers, and the real portals are at the sides. It is regarded as one of the finest examples of this type of long barrow. When it was excavated in 1863 thirty eight skeletons were discovered.

Places of interest in the Neighbourhood
17. Succour for the Weary (Ford)
19. Getting their Own Back (Winchcombe)

Food and Accommodation
Plenty in Winchcombe

The medieval cross, Stow-on-the-Wold.

21 Welcome to Stow-on-the-Wold

Ordnance Map: Cheltenham & Cirencester; Sheet 163 1.50 000
Map Ref: 1910/2580

Note: Stow-on-the-Wold is a delightful little Cotswold town with a number of minor curiosities.

For example, a notice in the church porch welcomes visitors in no less than eight different languages, bidding them to Enter, Gaze and Pray. In 1645 the church was used to imprison Sir Jacob Astley and 1000 Royalist troops defeated in battle by the Parliamentarians. This was the last major engagement in the first Civil War.

Stocks on the green are remarkable for the unusually wide spacing of the two leg holes, and by the west wall of the Unicorn Hotel there remains an ancient mounting block for the use of horse riders. The brass letter box of the Talbot Hotel is still inscribed "For Corn Returns". This is a relic of the days when the building was used as a Corn Exchange, and local farmers popped their grain samples into this box for assessment.

An ornate drinking fountain was presented to the town in 1896 by Piers Thursby Esq. and was erected on the site of a muddy pool where horses had been watered for centuries. In the centre of the town is a restored medieval cross.

Places of interest in the Neighbourhood
30. Gone but not Forgotten (Wyck Rissington)
31. The Crafty Mouse (Bourton-on-the-Water)

Food and Accommodation
Plenty in the town

22 The Itinerant Lady Rat Catcher

Position: The churchyard at Chipping Norton
Ordnance Map: Oxford; Sheet 164 1.50 000
Map Ref: 3120/2730
Access: Close to the path on the south side of the church and near to an ivy covered stump.

Note: In the churchyard at Chipping Norton there is a stone in memory of Phillis Humphreys who died in 1763, aged 58. The inscription describes her as "Rat Catcher who has Lodged in many a Town and Travelled far & near. By Age and death She is struck down To her last lodging here".

Places of interest in the Neighbourhood
18. The Rollright Stones (Long Compton)
23. The Remarkable Woollen Mill (Chipping Norton)

Food and Accommodation
Plenty in the town

23 The Remarkable Woollen Mill

Position: On the outskirts of Chipping Norton
Ordnance Map: Oxford; Sheet 164 1.50 000
Map Ref: 3070/2620
Access: Travellers leaving Chipping Norton by the B4450 towards
Stow-on-the-Wold will see on their left a strange building from
whose central dome rises a tall chimney. It is actually an old
woollen mill which has come to be looked upon as a folly by many
local people.

Note: In 1755 Thomas Bliss established a thriving clothing industry in this district. By the year 1870 it provided employment for some 700 workers, and the range of goods produced had been expanded to include Travelling Rugs, Shawls and Army Clothing in addition to ordinary civilian garments. It was in that year that the building was constructed with its spectacular chimney, huge clock and Jacobean style balustrades. Over subsequent years business declined and the mill was finally closed in 1980. At the time of writing (June 1988) it is still derelict, with most of the windows broken, but there are plans to renovate it and turn it into residential flats.

Places of interest in the Neighbourhood
18. The Rollright Stones (Long Compton)
22. The Itinerant Lady Rat Catcher (Chipping Norton)
78. A Link with Teddy Grisewood (Daylesford)

Food and Accommodation
Plenty at Chipping Norton

24 Memories of a Famous Jockey

Position: The King's Arms Hotel at Prestbury near Cheltenham
Ordnance Map: Cheltenahm & Cirencester; Sheet 163 1.50 000
Map Ref: 9700/2390
Access: Take the A46 north out of Cheltenham. The Inn is on the
left hand side going towards Winchcombe.

Note: A sign on the outside wall of The King's Arms Hotel reads as
follows –

> "At this Prestbury Inn lived
> FRED ARCHER the jockey
> Who trained upon toast,
> Cheltenham water & coffee
> The shoe of his pony
> hangs up in the Bar
> where they drink to his prowess
> from near and from far
> But the man in the street
> passes by without knowledge
> that twas here Archer
> swallowed his earliest porridge".

Although he died at the early age of 29 Fred Archer was Champion
Jockey of England for 13 seasons (1874-1886) during which he won
no less than 2748 races including 21 Classic wins. When he died he
left £60,000, a huge sum in those days.

Places of interest in the Town
See numbers 25, 26, 27, 28.

Food and Accommodation
Good food available at The King's Arms, and plenty of
accommodation in Cheltenham

25 A Famous Man for Killing Pigs

Position: St. Mary's churchyard at Cheltenham
Access: A stone bearing the following inscription can be found lying on the ground close to the pathway on the south side of the church.

> Here lies John Higgs,
> A famous man for killing pigs,
> For killing pigs was his delight
> Both morning, afternoon and night.
> Both heats and cold he did endure,
> Which no physician could ere cure,
> His knife is laid, his work is done,
> I hope to heaven his soul is gone.

I have read of another epitaph connected with his churchyard reading:

> Here lie I with my two daughters,
> Who died through drinking Cheltenham waters,
> If only we had stuck to Epsom salts
> We should not be lying in these here vaults.

Places of interest in the Town
See numbers 24, 26, 27, 28

Food and Accommodation
Plenty in Cheltenham

26 The Birthplace of Gustav Holst

Position: At No. 4 Clarence Road, Cheltenham
Access: From the High Street enter Winchcombe Street, opposite
to the Regent Arcade, and turn left into Clarence Road by the
entrance to Pittville Park.

Note: You do not have to be a music lover to enjoy a visit. In
addition to Gustav Holst memorabilia there is a fully furnished
Regency sitting room, a working kitchen and scullery. Many
people will find the servant's quarters in the basement particularly
interesting. The celebrated composer was born here in 1874. He
was the son of a music teacher and showed an interest in music at
an early age. His father wanted him to become a virtuoso pianist
but neuritis prevented this so at the age of 17 he began to study
counterpoint with G. F. Sims of Oxford. Holst's first professional
engagement was as organist and choir master at Wyck Rissington
church for which he received the princely salary of £4 a year. Later
he went to the Royal College of Music where he was awarded a
scholarship. He learned to play the trombone, and in 1898 became
first trombone player in the Carl Rosa Opera Company. In 1903 he
gave up the trombone in order to devote more time to composing.
It is for this that he is best known, particularly *The Planets* suite. He
died in 1934.

Places of interest in the Town
See numbers 24, 25, 27, 28

27 Montpellier

Position: In Cheltenham at the end of the Promenade, towards Gloucester. Free car parking is usually available in Malvern Road.

Note: Montpellier is one of the Cheltenham's most interesting districts. Opposite Montpellier Gardens is The Rotunda, built in 1826 as part of a Pump Room, and now occupied by Lloyds Bank and open to the public during normal banking hours. It is worth a visit to see the magnificent domed ceiling. It also houses The Napoleon Fountain, a fine piece of Italian sculpture with a chequered history. It may have been seized as booty by Napoleon's forces in 1800, only to be taken by an English privateer from the ship carrying it to France and brought back to this country.

In Montpellier Walk is a Victorian letter box and shop fronts upheld by a series of caryatides. Made of terracotta and painted white, these are copies of similiar figures from the Erechtheion in Athens and date from about 1835.

Places of interest in the Town
See numbers 24, 25, 26, 28

28 Cheltenham's Fantasy Clock

Position: In the Regent Arcade
Access: From the High Street or The Promenade.

Note: In the Regent Arcade is a weird and wonderful clock
designed by Kit Williams. Performing on the hour it is an unfailing
delight to children and of interest to many adults. It includes a bird
which lays eggs, creatures which pop their heads out of trap doors,
and a huge fish which blows bubbles.

Places of interest in the Town
See numbers 24, 25, 26, 27

29 The Devil's Chimney

Position: At Leckhampton Quarries, South of Cheltenham
Ordnance Map: Cheltenham & Cirencester; Sheet 163 1.50 000
Map Ref: 9460/1840
Access: By car the best approach is from the south. From the Air
Balloon Roundabout (A436) take the B4070 towards Cheltenham.
Pass turning signposted for Ullenwood on your right. After about a
further ¾ mile, opposite a house called "Mulberry", turn sharply
into a lane on your right. This is almost a U turn. You can park
your car in the quarry, a few hundred yards up on your left. Climb
the path on your right to the top of the escarpment. Follow the path
towards Cheltenham. You will see the Devil's Chimney on your
left after about ½ mile.

Note: The origin of this rock formation is obscure. According to a
local legend it rose from Hell, whilst many people think it was
created by quarrymen as a joke. But in the year 1900 S. S.
Buckman, an eminent geologist, expounded the theory that it is the
result of natural differential erosion over a period of many
hundreds of years. Some present day geologists support that idea.
Whatever its origin it certainly provides an interesting addition to
the landscape, and has provided a practice ground for local
climbers. In 1959 Gloucesteshire Mountaineering Club managed
to get thirteen of its members on the top at the same time. In 1986 it
was noticed that the column was in danger of collapse, and the local
authority spent £25,000 on its preservation. Climbing is now
strictly prohibited.

Places of interest in the Neighbourhood
Numbers 24-28 (Cheltenham)
38. He Died away from Home (Coberley)
39. The Source of the Thomes (Seven Springs)

Food and Accommodation
Plenty available in Cheltenham

30 Gone but not Forgotten

Position: 1½ miles N.E. of Bourton-on-the-Water
Ordnance Map: Cheltenham & Cirencester; Sheet 163 1.50 000
Map Ref: 1910/2150
Access: From Stow-on-the Wold take the A429 going southwards.
After about 2¼ miles turn left into a minor road for Wyck
Rissington church.

Note: The church is small but has a number of interesting features.
One, in front of the porch, is the grave of a travelling gipsy who
died in the village and whose caravan and possessions were burned
on a hill near the church in accordance with the custom of his tribe.
The stone reads – "In memory of James Loveridge of no fixed
abode (Gypsy). Entered into rest May 11th 1935. Aged 48 years. –
Gone but not forgotten".

Canon Harry Cheals, the priest who carried out the burial
service is also now "gone but not forgotten". He died in 1984 after
33 years as rector, and is remembered for the dream he had in 1947
in which he received explicit instructions for the creation of an
allegorical maze in the rectory grounds, representing man's
journey through life and based on a series of carvings in the church.
It took him five years to construct the maze with 7 ft. high hedges
and paths totalling 700 yards in length. Instructions to pilgrims
walking the paths included cryptic signs. Paths leading to a dead
end represented temptations and distractions. Eventually they
passed through a dark overgrown area representing Death, but
finished in a bright airy place, with flowering plants, denoting the
delights of Paradise. Over the years the maze became overgrown
and was eventually demolished to provide a building site, but
memory of the maze is perpetuated by a mosaic recently
constructed inside the church by John Bayliss. It shows the course
followed by the paths in the original maze.

Places of interest in the Neighbourhood
21. Welcome to Stow-on-the-Wold
31. The Crafty Mouse (Bourton-on-the-Water)

Food and Accommodation
Plenty in Bourton-on-the-Water and Stow-on-the-Wold

31 The Crafty Mouse

Position: At Bourton-on-the-Water
Ordnance Map: Cheltenham & Cirencester; Sheet 163 1.50 000

Note: For many years tourists have flocked to Bourton-on-the-Water to visit the remarkable model village at the rear of the Old New Inn. But a less publicised curiosity is the sign of the Mousetrap Inn. This shows a mouse in the act of coaxing a piece of cheese from a trap with the aid of a matchstick.

Places of interest in the Neighbourhood
21. Welcome to Stow-on-the-Wold
30. Gone but not Forgotten (Wyck Rissington)

Food and Accommodation
Well catered for in the village but at weekends during the summer it can become very crowded.

32 The Cross Carved by a Soldier

Position: Amidst the riches in Gloucester Cathedral is one that is often overlooked because of its size and obscure position. It is a small stone cross in a glass case and is situated next to the tomb of Osric, Prince of Mercia, in the Ambulatory

Note: The cross is the work of Lieut. Col. J. P. Carne V. C. who commanded the 1st Battalion of the Gloucestershire Regt. at the battle of the Imjin River in April 1951. He carved this little Celtic Cross from grey Korean stone whilst a prisoner of war, using two nails and a lump of rock for a hammer. The cross was used at services in the North Korean P.O.W. Camp from 1951 to 1953.

Don't forget to look at the misericord carvings in the choir stalls. These include one showing a strange monster swallowing a man, another a man embracing a donkey, possibly inspired by the story of Balaam and his ass. There is also one showing two dogs looking up at a fox they have chased into a tree, whilst an archer takes aim at the fox.

At No. 9 College Court, at the end of the Cathedral Close, is the quaint little house which inspired Beatrix Potter to write *The Tailor of Gloucester*. It now houses a small museum of Beatrix Potter memorabilia, and is well worth a visit, particularly if you have children with you.

Parking space in the Cathedral Close is often fully occupied, but there is a large car park near-by, at the end of Westgate Street furthest away from the town centre.

Places of interest in the City
There is much to see, and leaflets can be obtained from the Toursist Information Office at the crossroads in the centre of the City (see also numbers 33, 34, 35).

33 Gloucester's Curious Clocks

Position: The Town Centre

Note: Over a jeweller's shop close to where Northgate St, Southgate St, Westgate St, and Eastgate St meet there is a clock incorporating life sized effigies of national figures representing England, Ireland, Scotland and Wales. They are supervised by Father Time with his hour glass and scythe, chime the quarters and strike the hours on bells in front of them. The clock was made in 1904, whilst the figures, carved in wood and painted, were the work of a firm which produced figureheads for sailing ships.

In the nearby Eastgate shopping centre there is a modern clock which plays tunes and parades a group of puppets. Both clocks are very popular with children.

Places of interest in the City
There are a number of small specialist museums in Gloucester and details can be obtained from the Information Centre in St. Michael's Tower, next to the first named clock (see also numbers 32, 34, 35).

There are two car parks in Longsmith Street, opposite to St. Mary de Crypt church in Southgate Street.

 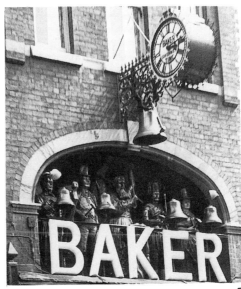

34 Robert Raikes' House

Position: Opposite St. Mary de Crypt Church in Southgate Street, Gloucester

Note: This fine timber framed 16th century house (now a restaurant) is where Robert Raikes, father of the Sunday School Movement, lived between 1768 and 1801.

In St. Mary de Crypt Church, opposite, is the font in which not only Robert Raikes but also the famous preacher George Whitefield were christened. Other curiosities in the church include a wall painting and an 18th century sword rest.

Places of interest in the City
See also numbers 32, 33, 35. (There are two car parks nearby in Longsmith Street).

35 A Pump with a Flywheel

Position: At Upton St. Leonards on the outskirts of Gloucester
Ordnance Map: Gloucester & Forest of Dean; Sheet 162 1.50 000
Map Ref: 8620/1490
Access: From Gloucester take the B4073 towards Painswick and
just after passing under the motorway turn left to Upton St.
Leonards Church.

Note: There is an unusual pump in the grounds of the school
adjoining the graveyard. It is still in use, and is operated by turning
a handle which starts a huge flywheel designed to keep the pumping
action continuous.

   Near to the churchyard entrance there is an interesting sun dial
with three faces.

Places of interest in the Neighbourhood
See numbers 32, 33, 34.
36. The Inedible Cheese Roll (Cooper's Hill)

36 The Inedible Cheese Roll

Position: At Cooper's Hill
Ordnance Map: Cheltenham & Gloucester; Sheet 163 1.50 000
Map Ref: 8950/1460
Access: At Brockworth (4 miles east of Gloucester) take A46
towards Painswick. After ¾ mile take lane on left signed for
Cooper's Hill. Parking space is available at foot of the Cheese Roll.

Note: At Cooper's Hill there is a steep grassy slope known as the
Cheese Roll, with a maypole on the top. The gradient is one in one
and each Spring Bank Holiday the hill is used for the ancient
custom of Cheese Rolling. A number of races are arranged in
which local lads and lasses chase cheeses (in wooden cases) which
are bowled down the slope. There is also one uphill race, and
dancing round the maypole.

   In the village of Shurdington (between Brockworth and
Cheltenham) there is an Inn called ''The Cheese Rollers'' with a
sign depicting the race in progress.

Places of interest in the Neighbourhood
35. A Pump with a Flywheel (Upton St. Leonards)
37. Crickley Hill Iron Age Fort

Food: Available in Brockworth at The Cross Hands or The
Gloucester Flying Machine
Accommodation: In Brockworth at The Cross Hands, or in
Gloucester

37 Crickley Hill Iron Age Fort

Position: Crickley Hill Country Park, 6½ miles east of Gloucester
Ordnance Map: Cheltenham & Cirencester; Sheet 163 1.50 000
Map Ref: 9360/1630
Access: From Gloucester take the A436 towards Andoversford. By
the Air Balloon Inn, at the top of Crickley Hill, take the left
turning (B4070) towards Cheltenham. After a very short distance
turn left again into the Crickley Hill Country Park grounds.

Note: Besides providing magnificent views and an ideal picnicking
site the hill is of major archaeological interest. There is a warden's
office with various displays illustrating the results of excavation
work, and depicting life in an Iron Age Camp. The site is open at
all times but overnight camping or parking are not permitted.

Places of interest in the Neighbourhood
32-35. Gloucester
36. The Inedible Cheese Roll (Cooper's Hill)
38. He Died away from Home (Coberley)
39. The Source of the Thames (Seven Springs)

Food and Accommodation
Available at Cheltenham or Brockworth

38 He Died away from Home

Position: Coberley church, ¾ mile south of Seven Springs
Ordnance Map: Cheltenham & Cirencester; Sheet 163 1.50 000
Map Ref: 9660/1580
Access: From Seven Springs take the A435 leading southwards.
After about 1 mile turn right into a minor road leading to Coberley.

Note: Sir Giles de Berkeley went to the Holy Land with Edward I,
with whom he became close friends. He returned to Coberley Hall,
becoming a Member of Parliament and Justice of Assize for
Gloucester, Worcester and Hereford. In 1294, whilst still in his
early 50's, he realised that his health was failing and made a will
leaving his peacocks and swans to his friend John Gifford of
Brimsfied. He also asked that his body be buried before the image
of St. Giles in the church at Little Malvern, but that his heart be
removed and deposited in the chancel of Coberley church. Less
than a year later he was dead. The spot where his heart lies is
marked by a memorial plaque, and his favourite horse, Lombard,
is buried in the churchyard nearby.

The church also contains effigies of Sir Thomas Berkeley and his
wife Joan. After his death Joan married Sir Richard Whittington of
Pauntley. In due course she gave birth to a son, Richard, who
became Lord Mayor of London, and gave rise to the legend of Dick
Whittington.

Places of interest in the Neighbourhood
24-28. Cheltenham
29. The Devils Chimney (Leckhampton)
39. The Source of the Thames (Seven Springs)

Food: The Air Balloon Inn (top of Crickley Hill)
Accommodation: Plenty at Cheltenham and Gloucester

39 The Source of the Thames

Position: At Seven Springs, 3 miles south of Cheltenham
Ordnance Map: Cheltenham & Cirencester; Sheet 163 1.50 000
Map Ref: 9690/1710
Access: From the A436 close to where it meets the A435. Free
parking space is provided in a lay-by.

Note: Several tributaries of the Thames are claimed as its source,
but that at Seven Springs is the highest and the one furthest from
the mouth of the river. The water gurgles from holes in a stone wall
a few yards from the road, on its northern side, to form a pool. The
spot is marked by a stone plaque inscribed as follows –

> "HIC TUUS
> O TAMESINE PATER
> SEPTEMCEMINUS PONS."

Declaring that the bubbling little river Churn, which rises here, is
the source of the Thames.

At the nearby crossroads there is a small round house which was
originally erected in 1840 by William Hall, a wealthy industrialist
and local squire. Its purpose was for people to leave parcels and
messages. These would be picked up by the passing carrier who
called daily and charged 6d for the service.

Places of interest in the Neighbourhood
24-28. Cheltenham
29. The Devil's Chimney (Leckhampton)
38. He Died away from Home (Coberley)

Food and Accommodation
Available at the Seven Springs Inn close by

40 A Curious Gate

Position: The village of Farmington
Ordnance Map: Cheltenham & Cirencester; Sheet 163 1.50 000
Map Ref: 1540/1360
Access: From the centre of Northleach take the minor road leading
in a north easterly direction and signposted for Farmington.

Note: Farmington is a delightful little village. On the village green
there is an attractive octagonal shelter erected in March 1822 in
memory of Edward Waller, squire of the village. It was originally
intended as a pump house but the pump has now gone. There is a
circular stone built dovecote but the most curious features are at
the church where the gate is made from 90 old horse shoes welded
together. Near to this is a tombstone in memory of Henry Ruck
which reads as follows –

> "A little while lifes journey done
> We too shall reach the blissful shore
> And dwell while endless ages run
> With those not lost but gone before."

Places of interest in the Neighbourhood
41-43. Great Barrington
48. Chedworth Roman Villa (Chedworth)

Food and Accommodation
Plenty at Northleach

41 "The Weak go to the Wall"

Position: Great Barrington Churchyard
Ordnance Map: Cheltenham & Cirencester; Sheet 163 1.50 000
Map Ref: 2060/1350
Access: From the A40, 3 miles west of Burford, take minor road
leading northwards. After Little Barrington branch right for Great
Barrington. Access to the church is by a pathway running beside
the grounds of a large house on your left. Drive slowly or you will
probably pass it without noticing.

Note: Against the churchyard wall is a long stone bench with
"elbows", moved from the church after pews were installed. In
olden days there were no pews in churches and the congregation
had to stand. However there was often a stone bench against the
wall for the use of the elderly and infirmed, hence the saying "The
weak go to the wall".

Places of interest in the Neighbourhood
40. A Curious Gate (Farmington)
42. A Fisherman's Prayer (Great Barrington)
43. The Left Handed Swordsman (Great Barrington)

Food and Accommodation
Pub food and Bed & Breakfast Accommodation available at The
Fox Inn

42 A Fisherman's Prayer

Ordnance Map: Cheltenham & Cirencester; Sheet 163 1.50 000
Map Ref: 2060/1350
Access: See notes on "The Weak go to the Wall" (no. 41).

Note: On the wall of the chancel in Great Barrington church is a
tablet inscribed as follows –

> "GOD GRANT THAT I MAY FISH
> UNTIL MY DYING DAY,
> AND WHEN IT COMES TO MY LAST CAST
> I HUMBLY PRAY
> WHEN IN THE LORD'S SAFE LANDING NET
> I'M PEACEFULLY ASLEEP
> THAT IN HIS MERCY
> I BE JUDGED AS GOOD ENOUGH TO KEEP."
>   Charles John Fitzroy Rhys Wingfield.

Charles Wingfield was the local squire and owner of most of the
buildings in the village. He lived at Barrington Park, built in 1738
to replace a house destroyed by fire two years earlier.

Places of interest in the Neighbourhood
40. A Curious Gate (Farmington)
41. "The Weak go to the Wall" (Great Barrington)
43. The Left Handed Swordsman (Great Barrington)

Food and Accommodation
The Fox Inn (At the end of the village towards Little Barrington)

43 The Left Handed Swordsman

Position: At Great Barrington Church
Access etc: See under No. 41.

Note: In a narrow space between the organ and the wall is a life
sized effigy of Captain Edmund Bray, dressed in armour with a
ruff. His sword is girt on his right side and he would have had to
draw it with his left hand. It is said that in his youth Bray slew a man
in a fit of impetuosity, but was pardoned by Elizabeth I on
condition that he always wore his sword on his right side to curb
any sudden impetuous action. Until 1734 the Bray family owned
Barrington Park, a huge wooded estate with a fine herd of deer.
The church contains several sculptured memorials to members of
the family. A particularly fine example by Christopher Cass depicts
Jane and Edward Bray, two children who died of smallpox at the
ages of 8 years and 15 years.

Little Barrington, only a short distance away, is a picturesque
village with the oldest and smallest Post Office in Britain. The
building dates from 1643 and the public space is only a little over
one square yard in extent.

Places of interest in the Neighbourhood
40. A Curious Gate (Farmington)
41. "The Weak go to the Wall" (Great Barrington)
42. A Fisherman's Prayer (Great Barrington)

Food and Accommodation
Available at The Fox Inn, situated at the end of the village towards
Little Barrington

44 99 Yews and 33 Tombs

Position: In the churchyard of St. Mary's church, Painswick
Ordnance Map: Gloucester & Forest of Dean; Sheet 162 1.50 000
Map Ref: 8670/0970
Access etc: From the main road in centre of the village. There is a
free car park on the corner of Stammages Lane, 100 yards past the
church towards Stroud.

Note: Painswick churchyard is famous for its clipped yews, most of
which were planted about the year 1792. According to legend these
number 99 and every time another has been planted to bring the
number up to 100 one of the older trees has died. Each year on the
Sunday following September 19th a traditional "Clipping
Ceremony" is held, but this has nothing to do with clipping the
yews. In this connection the word relates to the old Anglo Saxon
term "Clyppan" meaning to encircle. In the ceremony children
with garlands, accompanied by the choir and clergy encircle the
church holding hands and singing traditional hymns.

The churchyard also contains one of the finest collections of
table and pedestal tombs in the country. A leaflet, available in the
church, provides details of 33 of them. Many were the work of John
Bryan who died in 1787, and in contrast to the elaborately carved
tombs which he made he himself is buried in a plain stone pyramid
said to be a model in miniature of Caius Cestius' tomb in Rome.

Places of interest in the Neighbourhood
45. What a Spectacle (Painswick)
46. The Ship's Model in a Church (Painswick)
47. The Message of the Bells (Miserden)
53. Where the Wool Trade Flourished (Cranham)

Food and Accommodation
Plenty available in the village

45 What a Spectacle

Position: At Painswick, 8 miles south of Gloucester
Ordnance Map: Gloucester & Forest of Dean; Sheet 162 1.50 000
Map Ref: 8670/0970
Access: From the churchyard go out by the gate to the south of the church. There, on your left, against the churchyard wall, you will see some most unusual stocks often missed by visitors because of their obscure position.

Note: An act of 1350 required all towns to provide stocks for the punishment of vagabonds and petty offenders. The stocks of Painswick, which date from the 17th century, are almost unique. They are made of iron and shaped like a pair of spectacles. It is believed that the only similar stocks still existing are those at Dromore, Co. Down. They are sited near to the old Court House where the constable lived and could keep an eye on them and their occupiers. They were last in use in 1840.

Places of interest in the Neighbourhood
37. Crickley Hill Iron Age Fort
44. 99 Yews & 33 Tombs (Painswick)
46. The Ship's Model in the Church (Painswick)
47. The Message of the Bells (Miserden)
53. Where the Wool Trade Flourished (Cranham)

Food and Accommodation
Plenty in **Painswick village**

46 The Ship's Model in a Church

Position: St. Mary's Church, Painswick
Ordnance Map: Gloucester & Forest of Dean; Sheet 162 1.50 000
Map Ref: 8670/0970
Access: On the A46 2½ miles north of Stroud.

Note: Fixed to the wall at the back of the nave is a very fine model
of Sir Frances Drake's flagship *The Bonaventure*. It is about 7 feet
long and was made by a local man in 1885.

Places of interest in the Neighbourhood
37. Crickley Hill Iron Age Fort
44. 99 Yews and 33 Tombs (Painswick)
45. What a Spectacle (Painswick)
47. The Message of the Bells (Miserden)

Food and Accommodation
Plenty in the village

47 The Message of the Bells

Position: The church of St. Andrew, Miserden
Ordnance Map: Cheltenham & Cirencester; Sheet 163 1.50 000
Map Ref: 9360/0890
Access: From Gloucester take the A417 east. After the Brockworth roundabout fork right to Birdlip. At the top of Birdlip Hill turn right on to the B4070. After 2 miles fork left through Whiteway to Miserden.

Note: The tower at Miserden church houses a bell weighing over one ton. It is dated 1722 and bears the inscription "I to the church the living call, and to the grave do summon all" The small treble bell is inscribed "Come away, make no delay".

There are several interesting epitaphs at the church. One to Rebecca Gibbins who died in 1858 reads:

> "My glass is run, my days are spent.
> My life is gone, it was only lent.
> As I am now so you must be
> Therefore prepare to follow me."

A metal plaque on the grave of Samuel Horrell, a shepherd, bears the following lines.

> "From youth through life the sheep was his care
> And harmless as the flock his manners were,
> On earth he held the faith to Christians given
> In hope to join the fold of Christ in heaven."

This is situated on the right of the path shortly before the yew archway.

Places of interest in the Neighbourhood
44-46. Painswick
51. Don't Forget to Look Inside (Bisley)
56. Chalford Round House (Chalford)

Food and Accommodation
Plenty at Bisley

48 Chedworth Roman Villa

Position: One mile from Chedworth village, south west of
Northleach
Ordnance Map: Cheltenham & Cirencester; Sheet 163 1.50 000
Map Ref: 0550/1360
Access: Take the A429 running in a south westerly direction from
Stow-on-the-Wold. ½ mile after crossing the A40 near Northleach
take the minor road running westerly to Yarnworth and onwards to
the villa site. It is open to the public from 1st March to 31st October
except for Good Friday. Tuesday to Sunday from 10 am to 5.30
pm. (Last entry 5 pm.) For further information ring Withington
(024 289) 256.

Note: The origial villa at Chedworth dates from about 120 AD, but
there is evidence of alterations and additions continuing until the
late fourth centruy. There is a popular story that the villa was first
discovered accidentally by a gamekeeper trying to dig a ferret out
of a rabbit warren. The earliest authentic record of its existence
date from 1863 when a local archaeologist noticed Roman snails in
the undergrowth, indicating that the site had once been occupied
by Romans. The remains occupy three sides of a rectangle 120

A drawing of the hypocaust system.

yards by 85 yards and are regarded as one of the finest examples of a Roman villa to be found in the British Isles. Areas uncovered include good fourth century mosaics in the bath suites and dining room, latrines, and a kitchen with a large circular oven.

In 1924 the site was taken over by the National Trust, and there is a museum containing artefacts discovered during excavations.

Places of interest in the Neighbourhood
40. A Curious Gate (Farmington)

Food and Accommodation
Plenty at Northleach

Manticore, North Cerney Church.

49 Cotswold Beasties

Position: North Cerney church, 4½ miles N. of Cirencester
Ordnance Map: Cheltenham & Cirencester; Sheet 163 1.50 000
Map Ref: 0190/0780
Access: North Cerney is on the A435 between Cirencester and Cheltenham. The church lies slightly off the main road on the western side.

Note: The church at North Cerney has two most curious figures incised on its outside walls. They represent Manticores, and each is about four feet long. One is below the south transept window, and the other on the lower part of the tower. The manticore was a legendary creature with the head of a man having three rows of teeth, the body of a lion and the tail of a scorpion. Its favourite diet was naked men, but it was said you were safe as long you remained well-clothed. The figures are believed to date from the 16th century.

Places of interest in the Neighbourhood
50. The Dutiful Son who blew his own Trumpet (Bagendon)
52. Dalingworth Curiosities (Daglingworth)
60. Follies at Cirencester

Food and Accommodation
At the Bathurst Arms, North Cerney

50 The Dutiful Son who blew his own Trumpet

Position: At St. Margaret's Church, Bagendon, 3 miles north of Cirencester
Ordnance Map: Cheltenham & Cirencester; Sheet 163 1.50 000
Map Ref: 0110/0660
Access: From A435 (North Cerney – Baunton) take minor roads leading westwards.

Note: In the tower of the little church at Bagendon there is a memorial to Giles Parsloe who died in 1728. It is only unusual, indeed unique, in that instead of extolling the virtues of the deceased the inscription is entirely devoted to praising the son who paid for it:

> "A dutiful son I have left behind
> No man on earth could be more kind
> Than he was to me to my dying hour.
> He did for me that to his utmost power
> Nothing was me denyd that I would have
> In hopes to keep me longer from the grave,
> But God was pleased because he knows best
> To ease my pain and take my soul to rest."

Places of interest in the Neighbourhood
49. Cotswold Beasties (North Cerney)
52. Daglingworth Curiosities (Daglingworth)
60. Follies at Circencester

Food and Accommodation
Plenty in Cirencester

51 Don't Forget to Look Inside

Position: Bisley Church
Ordnance Map: Cheltenham & Cirencester; Sheet 163 1.50 000
Map Ref: 9040/0600
Access: To reach Bisley go east out of Stroud, turning right for the
village after about 2½ miles.

Note: The church of All Saints at Bisley contains an elaborately
carved font. Many visitors admire the carvings but miss the real
curiosity because they fail to look inside the bowl where two fish
are carved in relief as though swimming in water.

The churchyard contains a remarkable hexagonal erection
covering an ancient bone hole. It was built in the 13th century after
a priest fell into the hole and was drowned. It takes the form of a
''Poor Souls Light'' and is the only out of doors example in
England.

The Poor Souls' Light.

There are seven fountain heads in the village, all in a row. Each Ascension Day the local people observe an ancient Well Dressing ceremony. A procession of children bearing garlands of flowers gathers at the fountain heads for a service of blessing.

In George Street there is a lock-up with two cells, one for men and the other for women. It bears the date 1824.

Places of interest in the Neighbourhood
44-46. Painswick
47. The Message of the Bells (Miserden)
56. Chalford Round House (Chalford)

Food and Accommodation
Both available in the village

The lock-up, Bisley.

52 Daglingworth Curiosities

Position: At Daglingworth, 3 miles north west of Cirencester
Ordnance Map: Cheltenham & Cirencester; Sheet 163 1.50 000
Map Ref: 9940/0500
Access: Take the A417 leading north west from Cirencester and
fork left at Stratton. You will come to Daglingworth after about 1½
miles. There is free parking opposite the church.

Note: The church of The Holy Rood at Daglingworth attracts many
visitors who come to see the Saxon carvings. These represent The

Saxon carving.

Crucifixion, Christ Enthroned, and St Peter holding keys and a register.

However few notice two interesting bronze plates set in the floor of the porch. These read as follows –

"THE DISSECATION AND DISTRIBUTION OF GILES HANCOX WHO EARTH
BEQUEATHED TO EARTH, TO HEAVEN HIS SOULE. TO FRIENDS HIS LOVE.
TO THE POOR A FIVE POUND DOLE TO REMAINE FOR EVER AND BE
EMPLOYED FOR THEIR BEST ADVANTAGE AND RESIDE IN
DAGLINGWORTH."

Apl. 9th 1638.

"IN MEMORY OF GILES HANCOCK.
HERE LIES OUR BROTHER AND WE MUST AS WELL AS HE RETURN TO DUST.
HE WAS ENDEWED WITH WISDOM GREAT AND MADE UP DIFFERENCE
WHEN DEBATE TWIX FRIENDS AND NEIGHBOURS HE WAS ONE THAT SOONE
MADE UP THEIR UNION. HE LIVED IN LOVE DEARE TO ALL HIS FRIENDS
TILL DEATH DID LAY HIM HERE."

Apl. 1684

In grounds close to the church there is a circular medieval dovecote equipped with a revolving ladder to reach its 550 nesting holes.

Places of interest in the Neighbourhood
49. Cotswold Beasties (North Cerney)
50. The Dutiful Son who blew his own Trumpet (Bagendon)
60. Follies at Cirencester

Food and Accommodation
None available in the village but plenty at Cirencester

53 Where the Wool Trade Flourished

Position: At Cranham, near Painswick
Ordnance Map: Cheltenham & Cirencester; Sheet 163 1.50 000
Map Ref: 6810/1240
Access: From the A46, 2 miles north of Painswick, turn eastwards
to Cranham. In the village turn right into a minor road leading over
the common. After about ¾ miles the church is on your left.

Note: Cranham's connection with the wool trade in the 15th
century is indicated by two pairs of sheep-shears carved on the
outside of the west wall of the tower. There is also a table-top tomb
where wool sales were negotiated and the deals clinched by a
handshake over the "table top".
　　The church has associations with the Horlick family, of malted-
milk fame. One of the 6 bells in the tower was given by James
Horlick, and near to the churchyard entrance is an elaborate tomb
in memory of Joseph Alexander Horlick.
　　Inside the church one of the most interesting features is the
Triptych behind the alter. This is Flemish, of 16th century origin,
and the central figure (John the baptist) has 6 toes on each foot.

Places of interest in the Neighbourhood
44-46.　Painswick
47.　The Message of the Bells (Miserden)

Food and Accommodation
At The Royal William on the A46, or in Painswick. In Cranham
village food is available at the Black Horse and some houses
display bed & breakfast signs.

54 Refreshment for the Prisoners

Position: The lock-up at Filkins
Ordnance Map: Cheltenham & Cirencester; Sheet 163 1.50 000
Map Ref: 2350/0420
Access: Filkins is just east of the A361, 3½ miles north of Lechlade.

Note: The village lock-up takes the form of a narrow, windowless cell with a stout oak door in which there is a small grill for ventilation. When last in use the wives of the petty offenders it occasionally housed used to fill a teapot with ale and poke the spout through the grill.

Places of interest in the Neighbourhood
61. An Elevated Pump (Meysey Hampton)
62. Remembering Tiddles (Fairford)

Food: At the Lamb Inn.
Accommodation: At Lechlade

55 A Change of Usage

Position: 2 miles south of Stroud
Ordnance Map: Gloucester and Forest of Dean; Sheet 162. 1.50 000
Map Ref: 8420/0170
Access: From the west side of the A46 about 1¼ miles from Nailsworth.

Note: By the turning signposted for South Woodchester there is a round tower originally built to dry teazles for use in the cloth trade.

The tower has since been put to a number of uses including a general store house, and a home for pigeons. In 1982 it was converted into a private dwelling with a second smaller tower being added at the back.

Places of interest in the Neighbourhood
57. A Monster Copper Kettle (Nailsworth)
58. Who was Tom Long? (Minchinhampton)
59. Cubs for Hire (Minchinhampton)
66. Monument to a Martyr (Wotton-under-Edge)

Food and Accommodation
Plenty in Nailsworth and Stroud

56 Chalford Round House

Position: Beside the A419, 4 miles east of Stroud
Ordnance Map: Cheltenham & Cirencester; Sheet 163 1.50 000
Map Ref: 8910/0230
Access: From the A419, opposite the church at Chalford.

Note: The Thames and Severn Canal was opened in 1789 connecting the River Severn with the Thames at Lechlade. It was closed in 1933, but the round house at Chalford remains an interesting relic. It was built in 1790 to house the watchman whose duties included maintaining the towpaths and fences in his section and ensuring that the boatmen observed the company's byelaws. In this tiny, inconveniently shaped building one watchman reared a family of no less than 12 children. The youngest had to sleep on mattresses in the top storey where the ceiling was too low to admit the use of beds. Since the canal closed the tower has been used as a museum and as a craftsman's studio.

At Sapperton the canal enters a 2.375 mile tunnel, which when built was the longest canal tunnel in existence. As there was no towpath through the tunnel the mule or horse pulling the barge had to be led to the other end of the tunnel by a boy. Alternatively, if the barge was empty the animal would be taken on board. The vessel was propelled through the tunnel by bargees lying on their backs and using their feet against the roof or walls. This operation was known as "legging it", and prolonged pressure on the posterior sometimes caused a condition known as "lighterman's bottom".

Places of interest in the Neighbourhood
47. The Message of the Bells (Miserden)
51. Don't Forget to Look Inside (Bisley)

Food and Accommodation
Available in the village

57 A Monster Copper Kettle

Position: In the village of Nailsworth on the A46, six miles south of Stroud

Ordnance Map: Gloucester & Forest of Dean; Sheet 162 1.50 000

Map Ref: 8500/9950

Access: Enter George Street by the clock tower in the centre of the village. The kettle is on your left about 100 yards along.

Note: This monster copper kettle hangs about 15 ft above the ground. It is said to have been in its present position for over 80 years, and was at one time the sign for the "Copper Kettle Tea Shop". It has a diameter of 4½ ft and holds 80 gallons. Its estimated weight is over one hundred-weight. Perched on the knob of the lid is a normal sized kettle, and this has caused some local people to refer to it as "Little & Large".

The poet W. H. Davies died in Nailsworth, in 1940. Generally known as "The Tramp Poet" he is said to have coined the saying

"What is Life, if full of care
We have no time to stand and stare?"

Places of interest in the Neighbourhood
55. A Change of Usage (Woodchester)
58. Who was Long Tom? (Minchinhampton)
59. Cubs for Hire (Minchinhampton)
65. The Holey Stone (Avening)

Food and Accommodation
There are several restaurants and hotels in Nailsworth, and plenty of accommodation in the Stroud area

58 Who was Tom Long?

Position: Near Minchinhampton, 3 miles south of Stroud
Ordnance Map: Gloucester & Forest of Dean; Sheet 162 1.50 000
Map Ref: 8580/0130
Access: From Minchinhampton take the road leading over the common to a spot where six roads meet (north west of Minchinhampton).

Note: There you will see a multi armed sign post bearing a plaque which reads Tom Long's Post. The identity of Tom Long is a bit of a mystery. The popular belief is that he was a highwayman who committed suicide there in order to avoid arrest. But no-one seems to have left a record of his activities. Some people even say that he was not a highwayman but a local workman who committed suicide and in accordance with the custom of the day was buried at the nearest crossroad.

Places of interest in the Neighbourhood
55. A Change of Usage (Woodchester)
59. Cubs for Hire (Minchinhampton)
66. Monument to a Martyr (Wotton-under-Edge)
68. Hetty Pegler's Tump (Uley)

Food and Accommodation
Plenty available at Minchinhampton or Nailsworth

59 Cubs for Hire

Position: At Minchinhampton, 3½ miles S.E. of Stroud
Ordnance Map: Gloucester & Forest of Dean; Sheet 162 1.50 000
Map Ref: 8730/0080
Access: From Stroud take the A46. On the outskirts of the town branch left to Rodborough and continue over the common to Minchinhampton.

Note: Near to Minchinhampton church is the Market House which dates from 1698. On this is an interesting list of market tolls for the hire of cubs and other facilities for market traders. The word cubs in this context means cattle pens. There is also reference to payment to the 'Town Cryer', not to exceed 6d for each crying.

The church contains a brass commemorating James Bradley who was Astronomer Royal in 1742 and discovered the aberration of fixed stars. Mrs. Craik wrote her famous novel *John Halifax, Gentleman* whilst staying at Rose Cottage nearby in Amberley.

Places of interest in the Neighbourhood
55. A Change of Usage (Woodchester)
57. A Monster Copper Kettle (Nailsworth)
58. Who was Tom Long? (Minchinhampton)

Food and Accommodation
Plenty available in Minchinhampton

To be Collected in the Manor of Minchinhampton
by the orders of the Lord of the Manor

	£.s.d
Cubs are to be provided for the Sheep brought to the Fair at nor exceeding the rate per Score	0.1.0
Stakes and Ropes to be erected to tie the Horses and for each Horse tied too not exceeding	0.0.2
Standing For Goods offered for Sale 8 feet long 4 feet wide not exceeding	0.1.0

NB Any Person finding his own Materials to pay half the last mentioned Sum for the Ground The above Sums are to be paid before the Ground is taken Possesion of and the Cubs and Standings are to be returned in as good a State as when taken.

No Swing Show or Booth for the purpose of public Amusement will be Suffered to be Erected upon the Manorial Ground without the Consent of the Lord of the Manor and then in such a Situation and at such a Charge as may be agreed upon.

The Crier to be paid for each Crying not exceeding   0.0.6

60 Follies at Cirencester

Position: In the park of Cirencester House
Ordnance Map: Cheltenham & Cirencester; Sheet 163 1.50 000
Access: Entrance to the park is through the magnificent wrought iron gates at the top of Cecily Hill.

Note: The park contains no less than nine superb follies, but it is only open to the public for walkers and riders. It stretches for nearly five miles and none of the follies is near to the entrance gate.

The ground of Cirencester Park were laid out by Allen, 1st Earl of Bathurst during the years 1704 – 1735, assisted by his friend the poet Alexander Pope. Lord Bathurst wrote to Pope in about 1717 pressing him to come to Cirencester more often, and he promised the poet a special corner of the estate where he could do whatever he wished. As a result a stone summerhouse known as Pope's Seat was built at the junction of seven rides, and Pope spent much time there writing his poetry. The nearby beech trees, Pope's Beeches, are said to be the finest in England on account of their tall straight trunks, and were grown from seed specially imported from France. Alfred's Hall is a sham castellated ruin hiding a room where the nobility used to picnic. It was designed by Bathurst and Pope whilst the latter was at Cirencester recuperating from the strain of translating *The Iliad.* For many years "The Round Tower" was used as a shepherd's cottage. The Hexagon, an arched building with a cupola, was designed by Bathurst alone and positioned to command three vistas. Other follies include two ornamental archways known as the Horse Guards, Ivy Lodge, the Obelisk and Queen Anne's Monument, a Doric Column erected in 1741.

Places of interest in the Neighbourhood
49. Cotswold Beasties (North Cerney)
50. The Dutiful Son who blew in his Trumpet (Bagendon)
52. Daglingworth Curiosities
69. Curious Signs at South Cerney

Food and Accommodation
Plenty available in the town

Cirencester House and Park from the church tower.

Alfred's Hall, Cirencester Park.

61 An Elevated Pump

Position: On the village green at Meysey Hampton
Ordnance Map: Cheltenham & Cirencester; Sheet 163 1.50 000
Map Ref: 1180/0010
Access: From the A417, 2 miles west of Fairford take the road
leading southwards to Meysey Hampton.

Note: Visitors to Meysey Hampton may be intrigued to see a pump
raised high above the ground with a flight of stone steps leading up
to it, and once used to fill casks carried on horse drawn farm
waggons.

The nearby church has an ancient alms box hollowed from a
solid block of wood, and the lectern has the original chains used to
secure the bible against theft. In the corner of the churchyard is a
small building which used to be used as a watch house in the days
when new graves had to be guarded against the activities of body-
snatchers.

Places of interest in the Neighbourhood
54. Refreshment for the Prisoners (Filkins)
62. Remembering Tiddlers (Fairford)

Food: At the Mason's Arms
Accommodation: At Fairford

62 Remembering Tiddles

Position: Fairford Parish Church at northern end of the High St
Ordnance Map: Cheltenham & Cirencester; Sheet 163 1.50 000
Map Ref: 1510/0120
Access: Fairford is on the A417, 4 miles west of Lechlade.

Note: In the churchyard, 12 feet from the pathway in front of the church porch, there is a memorial to "Tiddles. The Church Cat. 1963-1980". In 1963 the verger took pity on a half starved stray kitten he found in the churchyard. He adopted it and named it Tiddles. The church became Tiddles' home for 17 years. Her

presence served the useful purpose of scaring away bats and catching mice. She was very well behaved and during sermons would often curl up on the lap of one of the congregation. When Tiddles died in 1980 a local stonemason carved the stone memorial which includes a realistic representation of the cat.

Inside the church are 14 quaint misericord carvings, but the lighting there is poor and an electric torch is a great help. They include one showing a dog raiding the cooking pot whilst the woman spins, another a woman beating her husband with a ladle.

Places of interest in the Neighbourhood
54. Refreshment for the Prisoners (Filkins)
61. An Elevated Pump (Meysey Hampton)

Food and Accommodation
Plenty in the village

The Jester's Tomb, Berkeley Castle.

63 Berkeley's Curious Tombs

Position: The churchyard at Berkeley
Ordnance Map: Gloucester & Forest of Dean; Sheet 162 1.50 000
Map Ref: 6850/9900
Access: From A38 take B4066 to Berkeley, and in centre of town
turn left for the church.

Note: Berkeley church has many interesting features, but for the
curiosity hunter the churchyard is particularly fruitful. Tombs with
interesting epitaphs include the Horologist's Tomb, with an
inscription referring to Thomas Pearce, a clockmaker and five
times mayor, who died in 1665 aged 77; and the Jester's Tomb of
Dicky Pearce, who died in 1728 and was jester to the Earl of
Suffolk. His epitaph is said to have been written by Dean Swift.

> Here lies the Earl of Suffolk's fool,
> Men called him Dicky Pearce,
> His folly served to make folks laugh
> When wit and mirth were scarce.
> Poor Dick alas is dead and gone
> What signifies to cry?
> Dickys enough are still to come
> To laugh at by and by.

Places of interest in the Neighbourhood
Berkeley Castle (Open to the public during the summer). For
details send s.a.e. to The Custodian, Berkeley Castle, Glos. GL13
9BQ or phone Dursley (0453) 810332.
Slimbridge Wildfowl Trust. 5 miles to the north. (Open daily,
except over Christmas, from 9.30 am until 6 pm or dusk).

Food and Accommodation
Plenty in Berkeley

64 The Temple of Vaccinia

Position: In the grounds of The Chantry next to Berkeley church
Ordnance Map: Gloucester & Forest of Dean; Sheet 162 1.50 000
Map Ref: 6850/9900
Access: From A38 take B4066 to Berkeley and in centre of the
town turn left for the church.

Note: In the grounds of The Chantry is a small rustic building which
saw the beginning of the end for one of the greatest scourges to
afflict the human race. It was in this building that Dr. Edward
Jenner, who was born in Berkeley, carried out his experiments of
vaccinating against smallpox in 1796, using cowpox as a vaccine. It
is said that Jenner was not the first person to try innoculation with
cowpox, but it was as a result of his experiments and the publicity
they recieved that the practice spread rapidly, and in 1980 the
World Health Organisation announced that smallpox had finally
been eradicated. Today The Chantry is a conference centre and
houses a museum of Jenner relics. It is open to the public during
the summer months, and the Temple of Vaccinia, as Jenner called
his rustic surgery, can be seen at any time.

Places of interest in the Neighbourhood
63. Berkeley's Curious Tombs
66. Monument to a Martyr (North Nibley)

Food and Accommodation
Plenty in Berkeley

65 The Holey Stone

Position: Near to Hampton Fields, north of Avening
Ordnance Map: Gloucester & Forest of Dean; Sheet 162 1.50 000
Map Ref: 8850/9990
Access: From Minchinhampton, take the road leading to Hampton
Fields. Just before you reach that village you will see, close to the
gate of a field on your left, a strange vertical stone with several
large holes running through it. Locally some people call it a Tingle
Stone, others refer to it as The Holey Stone. It is reputed to have
magical properties and in olden days mothers used to try to push
their sick babies through the largest hole to cure them, particularly
those suffering from rickets.

Places of interest in the Neighbourhood
57. A Monster Copper Kettle (Nailsworth)
68. Trouble House (Tetbury)

Food and Accommodation
Plenty available at Minchinhampton

66 Monument to a Martyr

Position: On a hill at North Nibley 3 miles west of Wotton-under-Edge
Ordnance Map: Gloucester & Forest of Dean; Sheet 162. 1.50 000
Map Ref: 7420/9550
Access: Approaching North Nibley from Gloucester by the B4060 the monument is clearly visible on your left. About 200 yards past the Black Horse Inn take the pathway leading up the hill. This can be very muddy in wet weather. Near the top turn right to the monument.

Note: This monument is in memory of William Tyndale who translated the New Testament into English. After ordination in 1521 he obtained the post of tutor to the two sons of Sir John Walsh at Little Sodbury Manor in Gloucestershire. In 1523 he moved to London where he lived with a wealthy draper called Humphrey Monmouth. There he began translating the New Testament into English. This, together with his outspoken views brought him into conflict with the church hierarchy, and to escape from persecution he fled to Europe. In 1525 Tyndale began printing his translation of the New Testament at Cologne, and later at Worms. Many of the printed copies were smuggled into England on merchant ships and found a ready sale, but any discovered by the authorities were burnt. In 1535, at the instigation of Henry VIII he was arrested and incarcerated in a dungeon at Vilvorde, near Brussels. There he remained for a year and 135 days before being found guilty of heresy. He was ceremoniously stripped of his priests vestments, and finally, in October 1536, he was executed by strangulation and his body burned.

Food and Accommodation
Available at The Black Horse Inn at North Nibley

67 Hetty Pegler's Tump

Position: 1¼ miles north of Uley near Dursley
Ordnance Map: Gloucester & Forest of Dean; Sheet 162 1.50 000
Map Ref: 7900/0010
Access: From Uley village take the B4066 leading northwards, up
the hill. After 1¼ miles you will see a sign on your left reading
"Uley Tumulus". If you leave your car and follow the path you will
come to the tump after about 300 yards.

Note: Hetty Pegler's Tump is the name by which Uley Long
Barrow is usually known. This name derives from the fact that in
the 17th century the land on which it is situated belonged to a
woman called Hetty Pegler, and it is said that on summer evenings
she loved to sit on the tump singing. When the Long Barrow was
excavated in the 19th century fifteen human skeletons were found.

Places of interest in the Neighbourhood
63. Berkeley's Curious Tombs (Berkeley)
64. The Temple of Vaccinia (Berkeley)
66. Monument to a Martyr (North Nibley)

Food and Accommodation
B & B accommodation is available at Hill House, on the main road
about 400 yards west of the Tump. Bar meals can be obtained at
The Old Crown Public House in Uley, and there is accommodation
at The King's Head.

68 Trouble House.

Position: On the north west side of A433 (Tetbury to Cirencester), about 2 miles north of Tetbury
Ordnance Map: Cheltenham & Cirencester; Sheet 163 1.50 000
Map Ref: 9130/9540

Note: "Trouble House" is a strange name for a Public House, but in this case it would appear to be appropriate. During the Civil War it was the centre of a bloody skirmish when Royalists drinking there were surprised by a party of Cromwellians. In 1829 two highwaymen (Mathias and Henry Finnel) were caught at the inn and subsequently hung. Two years later, Luddites who had been burning farm buildings and machinery in the neighbourhood, were apprehended there by troops and after a fight all were arrested and removed to Dursley gaol. Later the landlord, who had got into financial difficulty, hung himself from a beam. His successor also committed suicide by drowning himself in a nearby pond. Is it any wonder that the name of the inn was changed from "The Waggon & Horses", or that the inn is reputed to be haunted?

Prior to April 1964 there was a railway halt nearby, on the Tetbury to Kemble line. It was officially known as "Trouble House Halt". As there was no platform a beer crate was used to help passengers board and it became known locally as "Beer Crate Halt".

Places of interest in the Neighbourhood
Tetbury has a Museum of Police Bygones housed in old police cells.
65. The Holey Stone (Avening)
70. Of Clogs and Dogs (Hawkesbury)
71. A Three Decker Pulpit (Didmarton)

Food: Available at Trouble House
Accommodation: At Tetbury

69 Curious Signs at South Cerney.

Ordnance Map: Cheltenham & Cirencester; Sheet 163 1.50 000
Map Ref: 0500/9730
Access: From the A419 near Cirencester take the minor road
leading southwards towards South Cerney. Shortly after passing
the turning for Siddington you will see a castellated folly on your
right resembling a chess rook. This is said to have been built in the
18th century by a Dutchman who settled in the district. Continue to
South Cerney.

Note: In South Cerney village the most curious things are the
public signs. On the bridge in the centre of the village is one
reading "BOW-WOW", whilst in the western part of the village is
a street labelled "UPPER UP".
  On the door of the church a sign reads –

> "Enter this door as if the floor within were gold
> And every wall of jewels, of wealth untold.
> As if a choir
> In robes of fire
> Were saying here
> Nor shout, nor rush,
> But hush,
> For God is here".

Siddington folly.

Places of interest in the Neighbourhood
49. Cotswold Beasties (North Cerney)
60. Follies at Cirencester

Food: Available at The Old George Inn, Eliot Arms, or Peg's
Pantry. These are all close to the bridge
Accommodation: Plenty at Cirencester

70 Of Clogs and Dogs.

Position: In the ancient church of St. Mary the Virgin at
Hawkesbury
Ordnance Map: Bristol & Bath; Sheet 172 1.50 000
Map Ref: 7690/8690
Access: Fom A46 at Dunkirk take the minor road leading north
westwards. After 1¼ miles branch left to the church.

Note: Inside the church is a notice which reads – "It is Desired that
all persons that come to his Church would be Careful to leave their
Dogs at home and that the Women would not walk in with their
Pattens on". This sign was formerly in the church porch, but
recently it has been moved to a position in the nave.

Places of interest in the Neighbourhood
71. A Three Decker Pulpit (Didmarton)

Food and Accommodation
Available at Chipping Sodbury

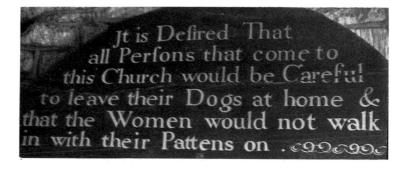

71 A Three Decker Pulpit

Position: St. Laurence Church at Didmarton on A433, Tetbury –
Bath Road
Ordnance Map: Swindon & Devizes; Sheet 173 1.50 000
Map Ref: 8240/8730
Access: Didmarton is on the A433. There are two churches and St.
Laurence is at the left hand side of the road as you enter the village
from the Tetbury direction. This redundant church contains
Georgian furnishings including a three tier pulpit. It is usually open
during the summer months. In winter it may be locked but the key
can be obtained from a nearby house, address in porch.

Places of interest in the Neighbourhood
Two miles away the church at Leighterton has a fine collection of
18th century chest and pepper pot tombs. 400 yards from the
church is a cemetery for Australian Airmen who died in World
War I.
70. Of Clogs and Dogs (Hawkesbury)

Food and Accommodation
Bar meals are available at the Royal Oak in Leighterton, and there
is plenty of accommodation in Tetbury

72 Elmer and Hannah of Malmesbury

Position: Malmesbury Abbey
Ordnance Map: Swindon & Devizes; Sheet 173 1.50 000
Map Ref: 9330/8740
Access: Entering Malmesbury by the B4041 from Tetbury the Abbey lies on your left.

Note: In the year 1010 a local historian at Malmesbury recorded the feat of a monk called Elmer who after studying the flight of birds took off from the top of the Abbey tower with wings strapped to his body. It is recorded that he glided some 200 yards before reaching the ground, breaking both legs in the process. He attributed this mishap to the fact that he had not been equipped with a tail, but there is no record of his repeating the experiment. For many years the event was depicted on the sign of a local inn, but that has now been demolished to make way for a supermarket.

   In the Abbey churchyard you can find the grave of Hannah Twynnoy who was killed by a tiger that had escaped from a travelling menagerie in 1703. Her epitaph reads:

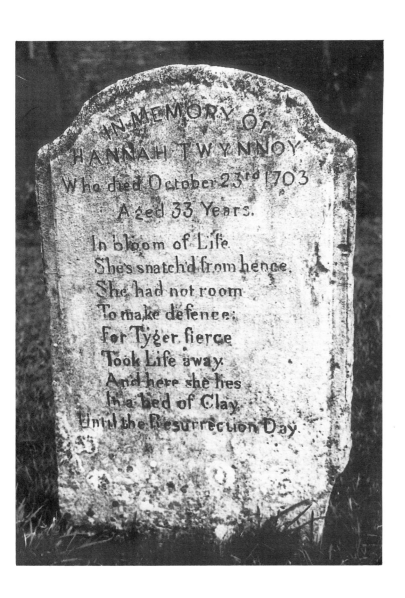

IN MEMORY OF
HANNAH TWYNNOY
Who died October 23rd 1703
Aged 33 Years.

In bloom of Life
She's snatch'd from hence.
She had not room
To make defence;
For Tyger fierce
Took Life away.
And here she lies
In a bed of Clay.
Until the Resurrection Day.

As you walk up the path towards the Abbey door the stone is on your right, about 15 yards back, close to a table tomb.

Food and Accommodation
Plenty in Malmesbury

73 The Slave's Grave

Position: The churchyard at Henbury, near Bristol
Ordnance Map: Bristol & Bath; Sheet 172 1.50 000
Map Ref: 5640/7880
Access: Take the A4018 near junction 17 of the M5 motorway.
After one mile join the B4055 leading to Henbury.

Note: In the churchyard of St. Mary's Church at Henbury is the
tomb of Scipio Africanus, who died in 1720. The memorial was
erected by the Earl of Suffolk in memory of his 18 years old black
servant, a freed slave. The headstone reads

> Here lies the body of Scipio Africanus
> Negro servant of ye Right Honourable
> Charles William Earl of Suffolk and Bredon,
> who died ye 21st December 1720, Aged 18 years.

In the 18th century much of Bristol's wealth was connected with
the slave trade. Whilst slaves were not common in the city some
merchants did keep them and advertisements in local papers of the
time record the offering of rewards for the recapture of runaways.

Places of interest in the Neighbourhood
Blaise Hamlet, a collection of cottages designed by John Nash and
now a National Trust property. Blaise Castle with its collection of
Victorian toys

Food and Accommodation
Available in Henbury village

HERE
Lieth the Body of
SCIPIO AFRICANUS
Negro Servant to y Right
Honourable Charles William
Earl of Suffolk and Bradon
who died y 21 December
17   aged 18 Years

74 Sally Lunn's House

Position: In the centre of the City of Bath
Access: From the Roman Baths proceed via York Street to Abbey
Green. The house is in North Parade Passage between Abbey
Green and Terrace Walk.

Note: This is the oldest house in Bath. It was originally built for the
Duke of Kingston in 1480, but the frontage was constructed about
1680 when Sally Lunn came to live there. She was a skilled pastry
cook and it became a very fashionable coffee tavern. It still
functions as a restaurant, and the history of the site as a
refreshment house can be traced back to Roman times. In the
cellars you can see Roman and Medieval foundations and a natural
display of stalactites and stalagmites. There is also a small museum
showing the original kitchen containing a faggot oven, Georgian
cooking range and various baking utensils.

The museum is closed on Sundays and open in the mornings only
during the week.

Places of interest in the City
Details can be obtained from the Tourist Information Centre in the
Abbey Churchyard
See numbers 75-77

75 Beckfords Tower

Position: On the brow of Lansdown Hill on the outskirts of Bath.
Ordnance Map: Bristol & Bath; Sheet 172 1.50 000
Map Ref: 7360/6760
Access: Leave Bath in a north westerly direction via Lansdown
Road. Continue up the hill until you pass Kingswood School on
your left (opposite the turning into Van Diemen's Lane). A few
hundred yards further on you will see Beckford's Tower amongst
the trees on your left, just past the cemetery. You can park your car
in a lay-by.

Note: This 154 feet neo-classical tower was built in 1827 for the rich
eccentric author William Beckford. Beckford was born in 1760 and
was only 10 years old when his father died leaving him an enormous
fortune, including an income of £100,000 a year from sugar
plantations in Jamaica. As his mother did not wish to send him to
school he was educated by tutors, and later travelled extensively in
Europe. He became an accomplished linguist, and his best known
novel *Vathek* was written in French. He spent vast sums of money
on the family house, Fonthill Abbey, in Wiltshire. This was an
extraordinary building with a 276 ft. tower which collapsed in 1825
shortly after Beckford moved to live at Bath when he retired from
politics as a Member of Parliament.

   In Bath he lived in Lansdown Terrace devoting almost all his
time to collecting books and works of art. He had Lansdown Tower
built to house many of his treasures. Before he died in 1844 he
expressed a wish to be buried in the Tower next to his dog, but the
family were unable to get the land consecrated and his granite
sarcophagus was taken to the cemetary at Lyncombe. However in
1848 the Bishop of Bath & Wells consecrated the land at Lansdown
and he was reburied close to the Tower.

Places of interest in the Neighbourhood
See numbers 74, 76, 77

76 Pay on the Nail

Position: In the covered market in Bath City Centre
Ordnance Map: Bristol & Bath; Sheet 172 1.50 000
Access: to market from The High Street, near Poulteney Bridge.

Note: In the 18th century a stone pedestal (known as a nail) was provided in Bath market, and is still there. Its purpose was for the settling of bargains. In those days counterfeit and "clipped" gold coins were in common circulation and purchasers were asked to place their coins on the pedestal for examination, i.e. "Pay on the Nail". If the vendor was satisfied he would pick them up. If not he would let them lie, a gesture of refusal. Similar "nails" can be seen in the Corn Market of Bristol.

Places of interest in the City
See numbers 74, 75, 77

77 Three Dimensional Carpet Bedding

Position: Parade Gardens, Bath
Ordnance Map: Bristol & Bath; Sheet 172 1.50 000
Access: Just opposite Bath Abbey.

Note: One of the most curious examples of gardening to be seen anywhere is provided by the municipal gardens at Bath. Each summer they prepare a bed in which three dimensional representations of popular T.V. characters such as "The Muppets", "Paddington Bear" and "The Wombles" are constructed of living plants. The bed is usually completed by mid

July and remains in position until mid September. The Parks
Superintendent tells me that the figures are made by constructing
shapes with mild steel rod and covering them with wire mesh.
These are filled with compost and the roots of the plants inserted
through the mesh.

Places of interest in the City
See numbers 74, 75, 76

78 A Link with Freddy Grisewood

Position: Daylesford Church
Ordance Map: Cheltenham & Cirencester; Sheet 163 1.50 000
Map Ref: 2430/2590
Access: From Stow-on-the-Wold take the A436 running eastwards.
After three miles turn right into minor road leading to Daylesford.

Note: For many years F. H. Grisewood was one of our best known
broadcasting personalities, but comparatively few people knew
that he was a Cotswold man. He was born in the rectory of the tiny
village of Daylesford where his father was rector. Freddy died at
his home in Hampshire and is not buried at Daylesford. But in the
churchyard there is a memorial cross in memory of his father,
Arthur George Grisewood. At the base of this a small stone plaque
has been added reading:

F. H. GRISEWOOD
of the B.B.C.
1888-1972.

MUCH LOVED

Also buried in Daylesford churchyard is Warren Hastings. Born
at Churchill, a few miles away, he died at Daylesford in 1818. In
1732 he went to India as an employee of The East India Company.
In due course he became Governor General but was recalled in
1785 and impeached for various offences. His trial lasted for over
seven years, but eventually he was acquitted on all charges.

Places of interest in the Neighbourhood
21. Welcome to Stow-on-the-Wold
22. The Itinerant Lady Rat Catcher (Chipping Norton)
23. The Remarkable Woollen Mill (Chipping Norton)

Food and Accommodation
Plenty at Stow-on-the-Wold

79 The Man who Rescued Robinson Crusoe

Position: In Stanway churchyard, 3 miles north west of Winchcombe
Ordnance Map: Worcester & The Malverns; Sheet 150 1.50 000
Map Ref: 0610/3230
Access: From the A438, where it meets the A46, take the B4077 towards Stow-on-the-Wold. After ¾ mile turn left to Stanway.

Note: Thomas Dover was born in 1660 and his career was as remarkable as he was eccentric. As a young man he cured himself of smallpox by having a blood letting and being placed naked to the waist in a fireless room with the windows wide open: he then downed large quantities of beer acidulated with spirit of vitriol. In 1700 he led a Privateering Expedition to Peru, and as a result became very wealthy. It was during that period that he rescued Alexander Selkirk from the island of Mas a Tierra. Selkirk had been marooned on the island for over four years when Dover rescued him, and his experience provided the basis for Danial Defoe's *Robinson Crusoe*. In 1709, supported by other privateers, Dover sacked the town of Guayaquil. The party took much plunder, and slept in a church were victims of the plague had recently been buried. Within 48 hours nearly 200 of the party became ill. Dover treated them by blood letting and an application of dilute sulphuric acid. Only 8 died. After returning to England and settling down he became famous for his "Dover Pills", a form of sedative which he invented. He came to live in the Cotswold village of Stanway in 1728, and stayed there until his death in 1742. He is buried in the churchyard in the vaults of the Tracy family with whom he was friendly. The vaults are surrounded by a low stone wall close to the grounds of Stanway House.

Places of interest in the Neighbourhood
  7. Bier at Broadway Old Church (Broadway)
  8. Broadway Tower
13. Memories of J. N. Barrie (Stanway)

Food and Accommodation
Ample in Broadway

80 Some Interesting Epitaphs

At Elmstone Hardwicke, near Cheltenham.
Emily Byron (a relative of the poet Lord Byron) who died 4.8.1855
aged 16 years.

> From scenes now shrouded oft with woe
> From life's depressing cares
> The youthful form that rests below
> The God of mercy spares
> Short was the span of life decreed
> Few were the griefs within
> The spirit from the casket freed
> Hath winged its flight from sin.

Here lyeth the body of Alice Little who departed this life 9th
January 1707, aged near 100 years.

> Death in a very good old age
> Did end her weary pilgrimage
> And was to her an ease from pain
> An entrance into life again

At Duntisbourne Abbots, 5½ miles N.W. of Cirencester. In
memory of William, son of William and Sarah Beames, who died
5th January 1799.

> A warning piece to all young men
> Who in their blooming age
> Mispend their time and know not when
> They must go off the stage

At Staverton, near to Cheltenham.
In memory of Wm. Harris who died 20.9.1835.

> My coffin, my bed my house and grave
> A little narrow room is all I have
> My body's rotten, but my soul is flown
> To take its rest in a world unknown.

At Brockworth, near Gloucester.
In memory of Joseph Baldwin.

> All ye that pass this way along
> Pray think how sudden I was gone
> Death doth not always warning give
> Therefore be careful how you live
> While you are living call for grace
> Death cometh stealing on apace
> Peace to this soul and may he rest
> in joys eternal with the blest.

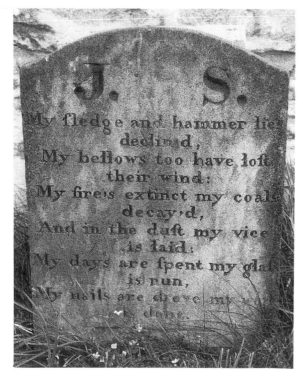

Epitaph to a blacksmith, Brize Norton.

Index